Written and Designed by **Golden Krishna**
Edited by **Daniel Shickich**

SPECIAL THANKS TO Gail Swanlund & Peter Kaplan

At tribute to

William J. Bowerman, William Dellinger,
Steve Prefontaine

the Golden Age of Long Distance Running.

IT'S UNFAIR. WRONG. EVEN. THERE SHOULD BE MORE TO THIS STORY.

I HAD THIS **FOOLISH** NOTION THAT I COULD do more for you. I thought that I could still teach you something new. I even hoped that my words would help you achieve your most arduous goal. But alas, **it's over**. This is **the end**.

If the greatest improvement occurs to the man who works most intelligently, perhaps we can improve this story by pretending that this end never happened. Perhaps instead of calling what's over, ***over***, I can take things back a step. Instead, pretend that it's 1969, the year we first met.

1951 1952 1953 1954 1955 1954 1955 1956 1957
1958 1959 1960 1961 1962 1963 1964 1965 1966 1967
1968 1969 1970 1971 1972 1973 1974 1975

YOU'RE 18.
YOU'RE WAITING FOR A VISITOR.

IN THE BACKWATERS OF OREGON, IN A TOWN called Coos Bay, you're 18 and you're waiting for a visitor. In a house built by your father after he returned home from Germany—where he served for the United States Army in World War II and met your German-speaking mother—you're 18 and you're waiting for a visitor.

You grew up in Coos Bay. It's a lumber town where leathery skin and scars show that the townspeople are descendents of the resilient folks that survived the long trek West in pioneer days.

Nothing about your childhood in Coos Bay ever stood out. You weren't anything special in the classroom.

On the athletic fields and courts you struggled; you would have been more helpful washing towels. And your peers, well, they made fun of you. You were the foreign, German-speaking boy and you never had any real talent.

Nevertheless, today a visitor is coming to see you because of what he believes is talent. He's coming to talk to you about something your parents think is a waste of time, something that, with one leg longer than the other, has never seemed like much of a natural gift.

The doorbell rings. You come down from your room. Your fingers tingle. He's here.

A MAN ENTERS YOUR HOME.

His name is Bill, but upon seeing him your elation turns to anger and frustration. Your hands clench, your blood boils and your mind begins to re-calculate your self-worth. This man is not the Bill you were hoping to see.

You were hoping to see someone else.
You were hoping to see **me**.

RUMORS OF YOUR SO-CALLED TALENT HAVE begun to spread. Now it seems everyone wants a piece of you.

Letters pour into your mailbox. There are so many it takes you an hour and a half a day just to get through them. The phone rings constantly. People even drop by your house in Coos Bay.

They all claim to understand you. They all claim to offer you something great.

THEY ALL WANT YOU TO BE A PART OF THEIR PROGRAM.

Sometimes you wish you didn't set that record. *Maybe then* these people would leave you alone. *Maybe then* schools like Villanova would stop writing you letters every day. *Maybe then* you could focus on getting to the place, the only place, you know in your heart you want to be.

But the people from that place don't call. They never really write either. Yeah, they sent Bill, but that's not who you wanted to see. That's not who you wanted to hear from. You want something—a phone call, a letter, or even just an acknowledgment—from the person whose picture you ripped from the local newspaper and hung on your wall: **me**.

1951 1952 1953 1954 1955 1954 1955 1956 1957
1958 1959 1960 1961 1962 1963 1964 1965 1966 1967
1968 1969 1970 1971 1972 1973 1974 1975

I'M 58: I'M MIXING RUBBER. ¶ A nail through the foot would work best, but these kids are too soft to put up with that, so instead I'm mixing lighter, stronger rubber. I'm making shoes.

There are hundreds of steps in 880 yards alone. My wife Barbara says that the fumes are no good for me, but if I can take one ounce off this rubber, it'll add up to 55 pounds over a mile distance, which means less weight to carry and more victories to celebrate for my soldiers.

Well, they're not really my "soldiers" anymore— that's what they were called when I was making boots in Italy during the War. We trained for mountain combat in skis at elevations over 9,000 feet, preparing to fight the German army. Now, these kids train near sea level for something that appears entirely different.

I left the Army with a Silver Star, four Bronze Stars, and a Good Conduct Medal. Now, I deal with skinny little runts who grow their hair too long.

People like **you**.

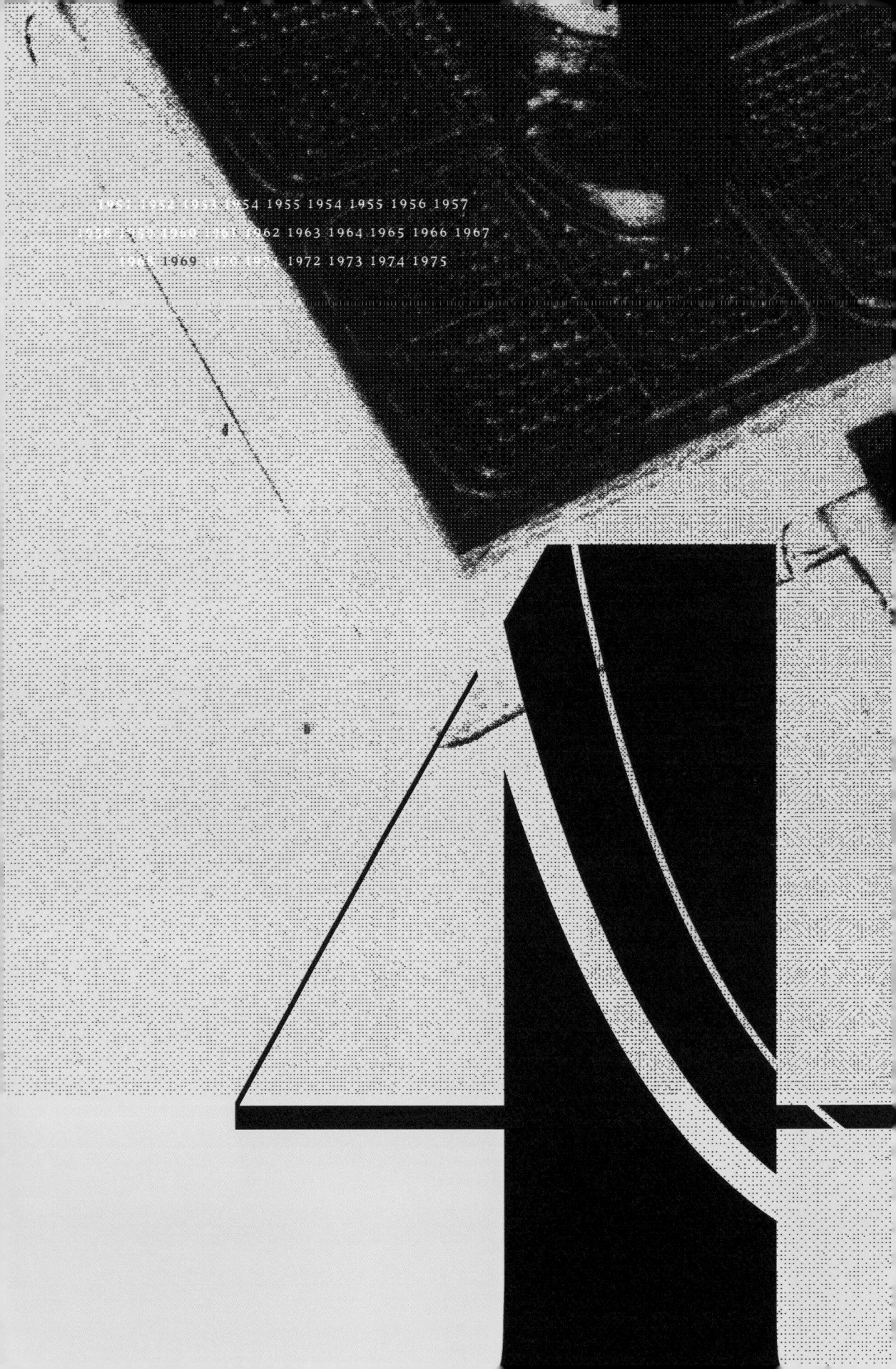

RECENTLY, I SOUGHT SOME HELP. SOUGHT another person to join me in turning these kids into the Men of Oregon. My new help and I have had a disagreement.

I don't bring kids to Oregon. I don't write to them. I don't make love to them. If they want a good education, then they can come attend the University of Oregon. And if they get into a better school, well, they should go there instead.

Bill Dellinger, my new help, disagrees. **He thinks** I should chase them. Thinks I should call them. **He thinks** that at times there is a talent great enough that it warrants that kind of attention. **He thinks**, for you, **I must.**

I don't do that kind of thing. If someone is interested in the University, he should write **me.**

A FEW YEARS AGO YOU FOUND FREEDOM. You found an activity that lets you escape the burdens of life and express yourself physically and artistically. It's a simple act, really: you just put one foot in front of the other. Simple enough for you to train and simple enough for you to focus your energy upon it.

This sport, running, gives you freedom. And when you recently ran 8 minutes and 41 seconds in the two-mile race as a high schooler, a new national record, the sport that brought you freedom brought you fame.

Forty colleges now chase you and the mail continues to pour in. Today, one of the letters is a handwritten note. You can barely even read it. "If you come to the University of Oregon," it says, "I have every confidence you could become the greatest runner in the world."

THAT LETTER WAS FROM ME

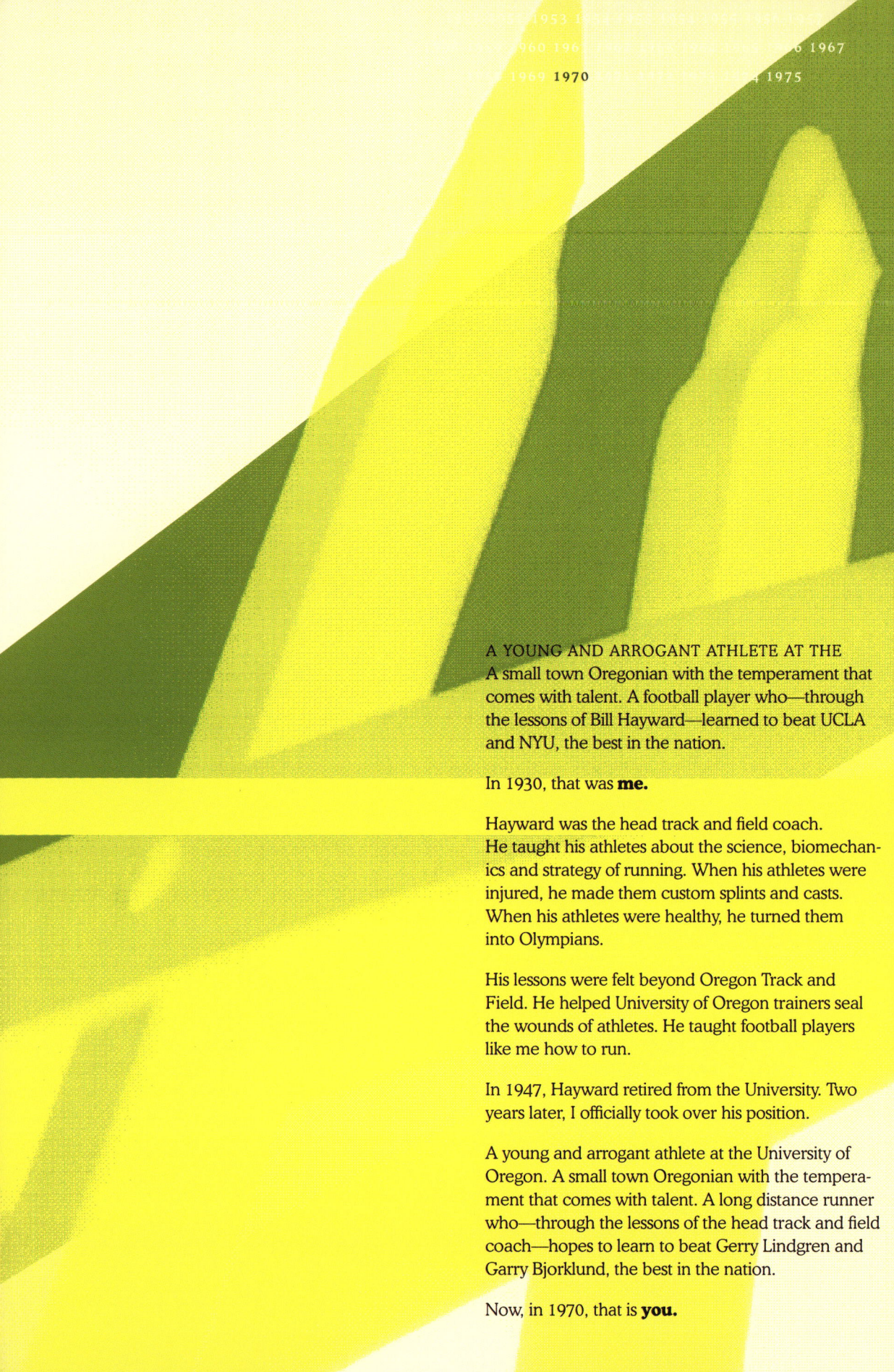

A YOUNG AND ARROGANT ATHLETE AT THE
A small town Oregonian with the temperament that comes with talent. A football player who—through the lessons of Bill Hayward—learned to beat UCLA and NYU, the best in the nation.

In 1930, that was **me.**

Hayward was the head track and field coach. He taught his athletes about the science, biomechanics and strategy of running. When his athletes were injured, he made them custom splints and casts. When his athletes were healthy, he turned them into Olympians.

His lessons were felt beyond Oregon Track and Field. He helped University of Oregon trainers seal the wounds of athletes. He taught football players like me how to run.

In 1947, Hayward retired from the University. Two years later, I officially took over his position.

A young and arrogant athlete at the University of Oregon. A small town Oregonian with the temperament that comes with talent. A long distance runner who—through the lessons of the head track and field coach—hopes to learn to beat Gerry Lindgren and Garry Bjorklund, the best in the nation.

Now, in 1970, that is **you.**

AT ITS THE MOST BASIC LEVEL, RUNNING OVALS around a 440-yard track requires your heart to pump blood, your lungs to process oxygen, and your feet to propel you forward.

Today there is a problem with one of those basic requirements. With the 1970 NCAA National Championships at Drake University—the most important race of your career thus far—just a few days away, there is a problem with your right foot.

It's sliced open. Blood is oozing from your foot onto the carpet of your hotel room. A gash between your first and second toe—later reported by newspapers as a swimming pool accident—is causing an unbearable amount of both physical and mental pain.

A man rushes down the hallway to survey the damage. On this day, at this moment, in this hotel room, this man is the person you'd least like to see: **me**.

YOU'RE OUTSIDE THE DRAKE UNIVERSITY track in your racing uniform and warm-ups. You're dressed to race, you're sweating as if you've warmed up, but have you no intention of running. Today, you're an actor.

Bill Dellinger dropped you off here half an hour ago. And despite the racing spikes in your hand, the sweat dripping down from your forehead and the look of focus in your eyes, it's all theatrics. An illusion we devised in your hotel room.

It took twelve stitches to seal the deep wound between your toes, and if you ran today, you'd tear apart the flesh in your foot. So today, you're here to fool people.

The three-mile national championship, your race, is scheduled in two days. But if rumors of your injured foot spread, and athletes noticed you limping, teams could flood the entries for the race and cause a qualifying round to be run today. A qualifying round that, if run, would tear your foot apart.

So today, you're an actor. And while to you the sweat is from pushups and the uniform is a costume, to other athletes, they are symbols that the rumors aren't true. Symbols that earn you two days to rest your bloody foot.

YOU STAND OVER THE SHOWER DRAIN, sweaty from the race, grimacing in pain. With your foot covered in blood, you and I both fear the worst.

WHAT WE ARE

MINE THE FATE

ABOUT TO SEE WILL D

OF YOUR RUNNING

You got your two days of rest, ice, compression and elevation. But those two days may not have been enough to heal a wound so deep.

I begin to remove the athletic tape on your foot. The patch job that we put together so that you could run this race has somehow withstood the brutal pounding and sudden and forceful flexes of your foot, but it may not have been enough.

The wrap comes off. Your foot is red. It's covered in blood.

But upon closer analysis, the flesh is intact. There's no permanent damage. Your worried face turns to a smile.

Now you can go think about your race. Now you can go reflect on the brutal three miles where Garry Bjorklund was defeated and Gerry Lindgren's NCAA record was surprisingly broken. Now you can go celebrate that you, the talented freshman with a temperament, won the race and are an NCAA National Champion.

ETER-

FUTURE.

1951 1952 1953 1954 1955 1954 1955 1956 1957
1958 1959 1960 1961 1962 1963 1964 1965 1966 1967
1968 1969 **1970** 1971 1972 1973 1974 1975

I'VE BECOME KNOWN AS THE JOGGING GURU. It started about five years ago when I introduced Americans to an idea adopted from the teachings of famed New Zealand coach Arthur Lydiard. Termed after an army command to run as slowly as possible and born out of a need to train middle-aged men with cardiovascular conditions, jogging was Lydiard's idea to keep the common populace fit and healthy. It was an extraordinary concept that I passed into American popular culture. Now, it's cool to jog in the United States. People never believe, until I explain it to them, how much life we've given back to them through this activity called "jogging."

The jogging movement has led to an explosion in interest in long distance running. And the celebrity that sits atop the trendy sport? **You.**

When I sent Bill Dellinger to your home this was expected. But *this isn't* why I wrote you a letter. *This isn't* what I had hoped to teach you.

I wanted you to join the dozens I have led down different path. I wanted you to become a member of a team I'm coaching in Munich: the United States Olympic Team.

But before you can win a gold medal in the 5,000-meter race, you'll need to qualify for the 1972 Munich Olympics and I'll need to teach you how to get there.

11

October 18, 1964. The rain poured down so hard that the runners' uniforms were soaked to their skin and an animated and packed stadium crowd replaced signs for their favorite athletes with umbrellas for protection. Two runners wore USA uniforms that day in the 5,000-meter race: one was my pupil.

Those were his third Olympic Games. Four years earlier, things had not gone well; eight years earlier, they had gone even worse. After the 1960 Games, he left the running circuit and went home to coach his local high school team. But he never lost his passion, and while training enthusiastic teens, he sought my help and re-trained himself from the ground up.

By 1964, he was smarter and tougher. And with a lap and a half to go at the Tokyo Olympics, he had the courage to steal the lead from those favored to win the race. It was a lead that was quickly stolen back, but a move that earned him a bronze medal.

Over a decade before that day he had come to me knowing little about running, and on that day in Tokyo I watched him run laps with the world's best. With him as my pupil, I learned how to teach distance running better. Now, in 1972, with him on my side, we can teach you to be an Olympian.

His name is a familiar one. His name is Bill Dellinger.

1951 1952 1953 1954 1955 1954 1955 1956 1957
1958 1959 1960 1961 1962 1963 1964 1965 1966 1967
1968 1969 1970 1971 **1972** 1973 1974 1975

You jog with *junior high students.* You volunteer at the *State Penitentiary.* You help *senior citizens.* But one thing has consumed your mind: **Munich.**

The Trials are just around the corner. And a defeat of George Young, the best American in the 5,000 meters, would allow you to not only capture a ticket to the Munich Olympics, but also send a signal to international doubters that despite your age, you're ready for the world stage.

George Young isn't easy to race. The *LA Times* Indoor mile was supposed to give you a chance to meet him, race him, and study his tactics. But he didn't show up.

"Goldarn!" you tell *Sports Illustrated.* "I wanted to run against Young more than anybody in the field. I wanted to test the veteran out."

You laugh.

"I almost said 'the old man,' but I don't want to make him mad and give him something to use against me when we do race. Besides, he's not really old. And I like him a lot. He's super intelligent. And very good-looking. And has a great family. And I hope he remembers all these nice things I'm saying when we do race."

1951 1952 1953 1954 1955 1954 1955 1956 1957
1958 1959 1960 1961 1962 1963 1964 1965 1966 1967
1968 1969 1970 1971 **1972** 1973 1974 1975

13 they

WERE HERE HOURS BEFORE YOU EVEN ARRIVED. WITH PICNIC BASKETS IN their hands, they sat on old wooden bleachers and talked about rumors, hopes and the new talent. For them, to be here is like for Apollo to be with Daphne. ¶ Now they're caught in the heat of the moment. **They stand and yell.** They scream in deafening unity. The crowd of tens of thousands sounds like a crowd of hundreds of thousands. ¶ If the noise—magnified by the walls of the stadium and rattling the bleachers—cannot be understood, they wear t-shirts with pictures and a phrase that they have come to embrace as their slogan: Go Pre. They're cheering for you, their prodigy. ¶ This is happening a few hours away from Coos Bay, in Eugene, Oregon, at the University of Oregon's track stadium, Hayward Field. ¶ To many, Eugene is the capital city of American track and field and Hayward Field is its capitol building. But to you, Hayward Field is the stage for your grand performances and great feats. Here, you have found a home for what some call your great talent, and today, this Cathedral of track and field is your path to Munich. Today is the Olympic Trails. ¶ The sounds of breathing and your thoughts of pain are masked by the roaring crowd. As you tear down the backstretch, George Young feels impossible to break. ¶ **Two laps left.** He's 10 meters back. ¶ The race started with a joke. One of your competitors removed his warm-up jacket to reveal a t-shirt with the words "Stop Pre" printed on the front. It's a play on the popular "Go Pre" shirts worn by Pre's People. Your People. Your fans. ¶ Now Young hopes to make good on the parody apparel. The crafty, 34 year-old veteran feeds off your pace. ¶ You keep your cool. The new pair of shoes I gave you earlier in the day feel light and comfortable. They are decorated by a symbol that has debuted today: a wing from the Greek Goddess of Victory. A Goddess named Nike. ¶ The crowd can't read the shoes. To them, the cursive 'n' looks like an 'm' and as they look at your feet they wonder, "Who's Mike?" But that doesn't matter right now. Right now they're witnessing history. ¶ You continue to push the pace. ¶ You push. And push again. Finally, an escape from Young. You break away. ¶ **One lap left.** The Hayward faithful see their prodigy all alone. No one is in sight. No one in America can match your speed. ¶ An already deafening crowd erupts as you cross the line. Three and one-tenth miles in 13 minutes and 29 seconds. You've set a new American record. ¶ A fan leans down from the stands and hands you one of the "Stop Pre" t-shirts. You put it on for your victory lap. ¶ You're 21 years old and you're going to **Munich**.

14 YOU HAVE A COMPULSION. A NEED.

TO GIVE ANYTHING LESS THAN THE BEST IS TO sacrifice the Gift, so you take the lead from the start and run 'til you have nothing left. To you that makes sense. To you, a race is like a work of art.

It works because in your mind you have no talent. **You have no talent, thus you have no limits.**

At Oregon there have been few problems with this strategy. After all, on the track at Hayward Field, no one has defeated you in any distance over a mile.

But now you're in Munich. About a week away from the most challenging race of your life. About a week away from facing the world's greatest runners.

Mohammed Gammoudi of Tunisia possesses a thunderous kick. An ability to sprint at the end of a race unlike anyone else in the field. At the Tokyo Olympics, where Dellinger earned bronze in the 5,000-meter race, Gammoudi nearly captured the 10,000-meter race due to his unbelievable last lap.

Lasse Virén, a 23 year-old policemen from Finland, trains in the woods. He claims the tranquility of nature gives him impenetrable mental strength.

So we've worked on a new strategy. We've taught you the chess game of the 5,000-meter race. Bill Dellinger and I have taught you to hold back, race patiently and run to beat your competitors.

But that isn't the race you're hoping for. You don't like the chickenshit of holding back; the chickenshit of running just behind another competitor, only to out-sprint him at the end. So you told an Olympic announcer you want the race to be all out. To be pure guts. And if it is, you're the only one that can win it.

1951 1952 1953 1954 1955 1954 1955 1956
1957 1958 1959 1960 1961 1962 1963 1964
1965 1966 1967 1968 1969 1970 1971 **1972**
1973 1974 1975

LASSE VIRÉN IS IN FIFTH PLACE. Today, about a week before the 5,000-meter race, Virén is participating in the other great Olympic long distance race: the 10,000-meters.

Someone in the front of the pack slows down. Chaos ensues. Virén nearly trips over the runner in front of him. For the runner directly behind Virén, an American named Frank Shorter, the change of pace is too much: he sticks out his arms to regain his balance and incidentally shoves Virén to the ground. A third runner, Mohammed Gammoudi, gets his leg trapped below Virén's chest and he topples over.

The pack proceeds.

A sneeze can be the difference between winning and losing an Olympic race. A small move can win or lose a medal. Now Virén and Gammoudi lay on the ground.

Gammoudi is hurt. He lays in fetal position. He puts his head down and mourns his Olympic loss. But Virén gets up instantly. He chases the pack. Those runs in the woods have prepared him for this.

Gammoudi slowly rises. The crowd cheers. But he is nowhere near the pack. He has nowhere near the mental toughness of Virén.

As a runner from the UK sets the pace, Virén sits within a close pack behind. He plays the chess game. Gammoudi, running alone much further behind, drops out of the race.

WITH TWO AND A HALF MILES LEFT VIRÉN MOVES INTO THIRD AND THEN, SURPRISINGLY, TAKES THE LEAD.

Seven laps left. Virén seems unaffected by his earlier fall. He surges.

Two laps left. Virén gets passed by three runners. He passes them back with a speed no one can match.

He wins. He sets **an Olympic record.**

16

My eyelids are closing themselves. I'm exhausted. A warm bed sounds…

Someone is pounding at the door.

I might be the head coach for the US team at these Olympic Games, but an athlete's late-night request for more towels can wait. I open the door anyway.

An exhausted, worried athlete stands before me. He tells me he's Israeli. He tells me there are Arabs in his building at the Olympic Village.

I can barely stay awake. "Well, tell them to get out," I say.

His horrified face reveals the problem isn't so simple. He tells me they have guns. He tells me they've shot and killed his fellow Israeli athletes.

17

You're at the greatest moment of your career. You've fulfilled a childhood dream and made it to the Olympics. But you feel *sick*. **Horrible**. Disgusted. The Olympic Games are to continue despite the fact that a terrorist group kidnapped Israeli athletes and a rescue attempt by the German government resulted in the death of everyone involved.

The man who angered you years ago knows you need to leave. You need to escape the madness. So Bill Dellinger drives you away into the Austrian Alps. And to make sure you don't run like mad to ease your pain, he jogs with you.

Although you volunteered to be the first on a flight home if the Olympic Games were cancelled, Bill realizes you're also frustrated for pragmatic reasons. A delay in the Olympic Games means Lasse Virén gets more time to rest between the 10,000-meter race where he won gold and the 5,000-meter race where he aims to beat **you**.

18

A MAN IN A JACKET RA STARTING

YOUR PALMS SWEAT.
YOUR VISION BLURS.
Your heart explodes inside your chest.

There is something humbling about where you stand. The starting line is a place where all are equal. It is a place where what matters isn't what has happened before stepping up to the line; rather, what will happen after the line is crossed.

Preliminary heats were held to narrow this field down to the world's thirteen best runners.

In your heat your pace was so strong that when you were passed in the final 200 meters, the man who edged you set an Olympic record. But as I already said, that does not matter at the starting line.

A white cloud of smoke emerges as the starting gun erupts.

The aura of the moment takes over. Laps pass without thought. The group's pace is slow, even pedestrian.

BLUE ISES THE GUN.

Lasse Virén watches you closely from behind. He knows…

You're trapped. You're stuck in a pack of international all-stars. Unable to move…

You're trapped. The raucous crowd in Munich, Germany drowns out your inner thoughts. You need to break free, but…

In 1954, a British medical student made headlines around the world for being the first human to break four minutes in a mile race. Just weeks ago, in 1972, you have made headlines around the world for claiming that you'd run a four-minute mile to end, and to win, this three-mile race.

Lasse Virén peers forward. He is well aware of those headlines. He is well aware of your claim.

A mile remains. An opening appears. You break free. You take the lead.

Three laps left. Virén passes five runners and runs directly behind you. He breathes down your neck.

HE FEEDS OFF

Two laps left. Virén passes you. You pass him back.

One lap left. Virén passes you with authority: A move to declare his superiority. Mohammed Gammoudi follows him.

For years you've been training for this Olympic race. For years you've learned the strategies I've taught you. So you know, as I've taught you, that everything you need is already inside. You know that there are times when the chess game ends and you have to rely on your own judgment. So you rely on your inner instincts, your inner needs. You don't sit back and hope for a silver. You chase gold. You chase Virén.

200 meters left. Virén increases the pace. You give it everything. Your eyes widen as your mind fills with hope and your body fills with adrenaline.

100 meters left. Virén pulls away. So does Gammoudi. You bow your head and pump your arms furiously hoping for more inner strength.

20 meters left. You're in third. Your legs refuse to move. They burn, filling with acid that your body hopes will help them receive oxygen for a final push. But it's too late. Scotsman Ian Stewart reveals his thunderous kick and passes you, claiming the bronze medal.

YOUR PAC E.

You cross the finish line. No gold. No silver. No bronze. You've crossed the line with nothing.

IT'S

COLD.

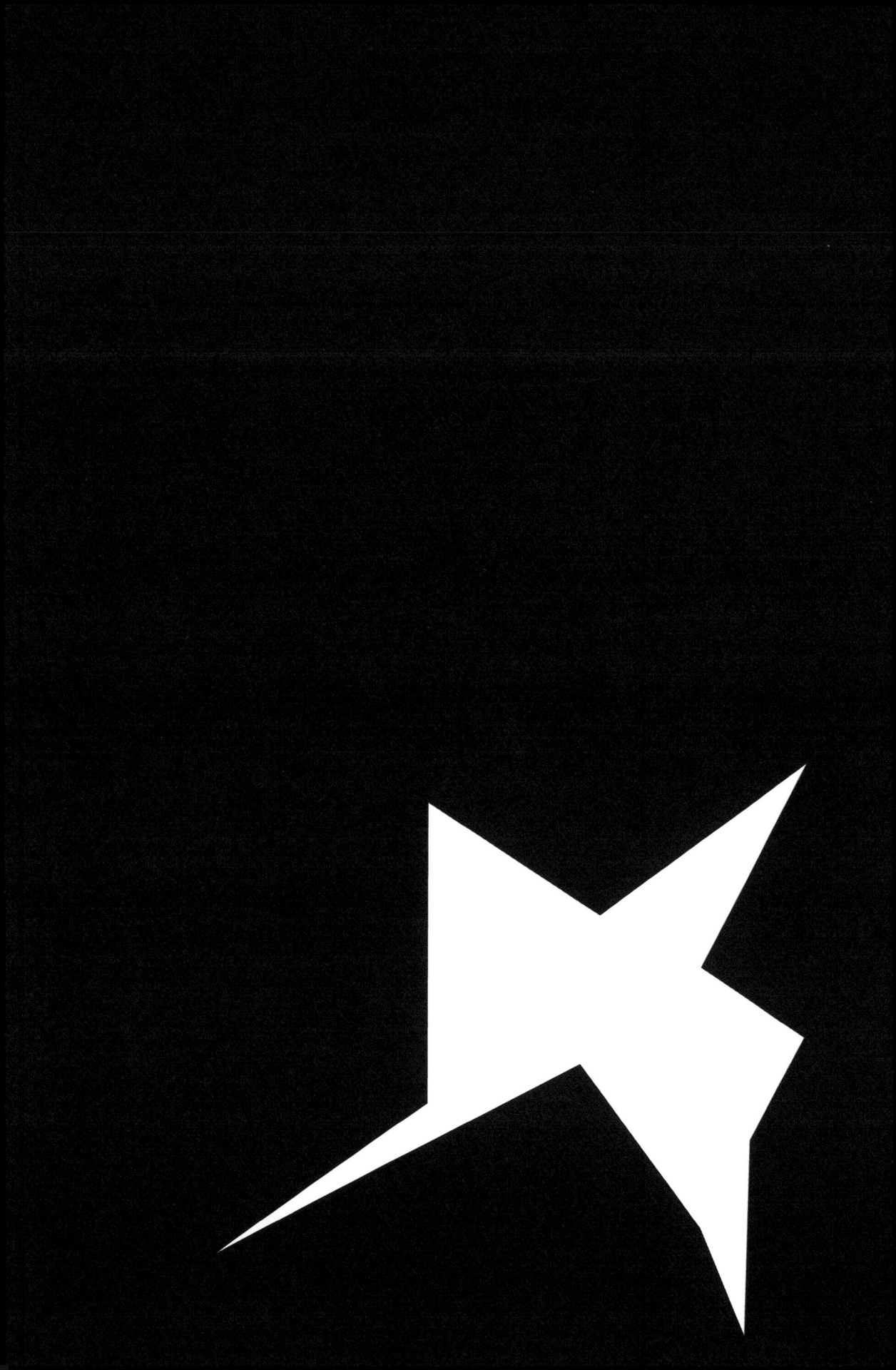

YOU'RE LONELY.

Lobo, a German Shepherd rescued from a local shelter, feels like your only friend.

The path to Munich meant large crowds, autographs and a celebrity status. Now you sit alone in your trailer, forgotten by the world in a non-Olympic year. If they recognize you on the street, strangers ask, "What happened to you?"

This trailer has become home. The Amateur Athletic Union, or the AAU, is the governing body for track and field athletes. In order to be eligible for the next Olympics, you must remain an amateur and a member of the AAU. That means surviving on their $3 per day allowance.

It's a depressing life, really. You may have been the world's best-known long distance runner, but now you live on food stamps and call a trailer your home.

A FEW MONTHS AGO I saw one of the greatest performances in running that I have ever seen. A young man returned to the country of his mother's origin and showed courage that takes some athletes three Olympics to scour up. He ran his last mile in an incredible 4 minutes and 6 seconds. Lasse Virén just happened to run it in 4 minutes and 2 seconds.

Before he was sent off to battle in the war-minded Sparta, a mother would hand a shield to her son and ask him to return from battle with that shield raised in victory or return home dead upon it, having given everything he had in battle. Either of these outcomes was considered honorable; any other outcome brought shame to the family.

This is not Sparta. This is Oregon. But tell me, would a Spartan mother—a member of one of the most judgmental societies in human history—not be proud of what you did in Munich?

A TRAGEDY CAN MARK A MAN.
But sometimes the most interesting part of a story isn't when a man falls; instead, it's what happens to him when he gets up.

For you, something was gone. An edge that once made you unstoppable was lost.

After two mediocre performances following Munich, you told the papers it doesn't matter if you win.

You thought that a third poor performance would mean walking out the door after the race. You thought it would mean never running again. A poor performance would result in saying goodbye to the sport, your fans and your chances of an Olympic medal in the next Games.

But then *something* happened: Lasse Virén came to town. He came to race you at an indoor meet in Los Angeles called the Sunkist Invitational.

And in an event stacked with talent, a race featuring two Olympic champions, *something* clicked. *Something* new.

Yes, Virén had claimed that he had reduced his training from his Olympic routine of 20 miles a day to 30 miles a week, but that didn't matter when you burned by him and lapped your competitors in the indoor two-mile race. You found *something* new that day. On a day where you nearly retired, you surpassed a breaking point by defeating your Munich rival.

It's been a few months since then and you've adopted a new attitude that is expressed in more ways than running. A thick mustache, long hair and sideburns embody more than your newly discovered rebellious and wise attitude. They are symbols of a new spirit within you.

And today, at the 1973 NCAA Track and Field Championships, you showed that spirit by surpassing your own NCAA record and claiming another national title in your last collegiate track season. The scoreboard reads:

1951 1952 1953 1954 1955 1954 1955 1
1958 1959 1960 1961 1962 1963 1964 1966
1968 1969 1970 1971 1972 **1973** 197

5TH **MANH**
4TH **W. ST.**
3RD **COLO**
2ND **COLO**
1ST **PRE**

Today, you're back on top.

23

ELECT

,

THIS PLACE IS RICH.

WHEN A PERSON COMES HERE,

HE FEELS IT INSIDE,

His crowded thoughts become clear and his blood rushes through his veins. This place has granted miracles and given birth to saints. This place is **Hayward Field.**

Today, *its stands are crumbling*. Today, its seats are shaky. A fire marshal has deemed an entire grandstand unsafe.

For hundreds of years, men laid down their arms to show their moral advancement by fighting their wars on tracks like Hayward instead of battlefields; they used competition—running, jumping and throwing—to conquer their enemies instead of kidnapping and killing. The murder of Israeli athletes at the Munich Olympics showed that this generation has not yet understood this ideal. Dealing with that situation firsthand and the chaos that ensued afterward has placed a great burden on my mind and body.

I will no longer coach. Not only do I lack the energy, but I also have a short time to do something for the future of Hayward Field.

My last and best contribution I can give the University of Oregon is to put all of my energies into getting a facility for the athletes, students and community. Since we do not have the financial means to fix it professionally, I will personally rebuild Hayward Field.

Rebuilding will require strong wood, hard work, and above all, money. Last year, we raised $8,000 for rebuilding materials. At that rate, it'll take 750 years to purchase the necessary supplies. The Oregon Track Club and I can find more donors, but not enough to fund the entire process. However, there is still a way to save this place: **you**.

LOBO RUNS TO YOU, his tail waging with the enthusiasm of the Hayward Field faithful when you're running down the homestretch. You're not finishing a race, however, rather coming home from a fast run through the trails of Eugene. Drenched in sweat, you grab your mail from your mailbox and sit down on the three stairs leading to your trailer's front door.

Another letter form the International Track Association, the new track circuit. They are a professional organization of elite athletes touring the world for money. They need a superstar to draw bigger crowds. They need you.

This letter is ITA's biggest offer thus far: $100,000 a year. Certainly, living on $3 a day has been tough. And now that you've graduated, scholarship money can't help with odds and ends anymore. Even a position at the startup company Blue Ribbon Sports that paid $5,000 a year got you in trouble with the AAU. Amateur athletes, the only ones that the US will send to the Olympics, aren't supposed to earn money for their Olympic talents.

You love the idea of running at Montreal in '76, the next Olympic Games. You get a shot at beating Virén on a world stage. You get a shot at earning a gold medal.

You hate the idea of running at Montreal in '76, the next Olympic Games. It requires food stamps, living in a trailer, and above all, abiding by the rules of a governing body that makes you wish you had no love for your country.

Lobo's tail continues to wag back and forth.

The ITA can wait. There is someone far more important that needs your help.

YOU'RE IN GERMANY.

You're walking to an AAU team meeting with Dave Wottle. He's been labeled lanky and square. But with you, he feels *invincible*. With you, he is a *rebel*.

The two of you have been running beyond the AAU's control. Although scheduled to be a part of an international amateur tour, the two of you felt there was something more important: **Hayward Field**.

My efforts with the Oregon Track Club brought in hundreds of thousands in donations, but still not enough to rebuild Hayward. So an idea to save the stadium by hosting a meet became a reality when you picked up a phone and challenged Dave Wottle to a mile race.

Five days later, instead of flying to Scandinavia, Wottle came to Eugene. Your plan wasn't to beat each other, rather it was to chase the mile world record.

The idea brought a sold-out crowd to Hayward Field. And at this meet, the Oregon Restoration, Wottle blew by you with 220 yards left and finished the mile race in 3 minutes and 53 seconds. The race put Wottle a mere 2 seconds shy of the world record, and more importantly, brought enough money to save Hayward Field.

Touring Europe reveals the AAU's deceptive schemes. After meets, European athletes are handed their appearance money while the money you earn goes straight to AAU officials. While European athletes party at local hot spots, you try to find the cheapest beer in town.

Things are different in Finland. There, locals open their doors to you for home-cooked meals, beds and saunas. There, in the home country of Lasse Virén, the people feel like Oregonians.

To thank them for their hospitality, you invite them back to Oregon. You call up local friends, Finnish track stars and even get Lasse Virén to agree to a pre-Montreal Olympic tune-up; a mini tour of the Pacific Northwest to race America's best. As defacto controllers of international competition on US soil, the AAU is offended, disgruntled and upset. But an outcry of public support leaves them with no choice: they sanction your 1975 tour.

Virén pulls out. Frank Shorter, at home sick with a swollen jaw from pulled wisdom teeth, can't resist. He fills in for Virén in the 5,000-meter finale of your brilliant tour.

Afterwards, the two of you celebrate with the Fins, you give Frank a ride home and then drive down a twisty, mountain road.

Paul Geis limps out of Montreal's Olympic Stadium. His legs are sore, his mind is numb from pushing his body to its limits, and his ears are ringing from the sounds of the Finnish national anthem.

***Oi maamme, Suomi, synnyinmaa!*ʼ**

Lasse Virén has done the unthinkable. A domination of the 5,000 and 10,000 meters. A fifth-placed finish in the Olympic marathon. Inhuman results.

Geis had raced 'til he had no more gas. Though from the wretched television coverage, it appeared as though all he needed was a little sprint to pass Virén, he could not compete with Virén's incredible speed and finished 12th in the 5,000 meters.

Watching the Olympics on television from Oregon has not been easy for me. But being in Montreal without you would have been impossible.

28

My arm is shaking. Barbara was
right about those fumes.

After dropping off Frank in 1975, something happened
down that winding road that is still too painful to recall.
An end to this story that churns in my stomach like rotten meat and never quite goes away.

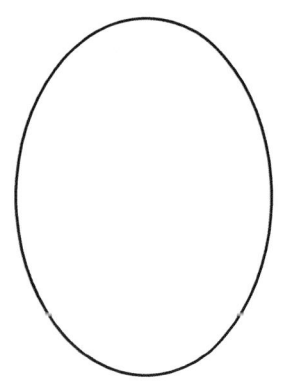
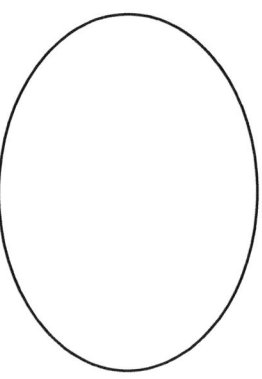

But this story's peak is strong. Its lessons are timeless.

Lessons that caused the AAU to lose its power in 1978.

Lessons that caused a 16-year old kid to ask me yesterday, twenty-some years since the car crash, what it was like "to coach Pre." This kid, never having met his hero, seen him run or even been alive before 1980, had motivated himself to become a hard-working, critical-thinking dreamer because of this story.

And that is what makes this story worth telling.

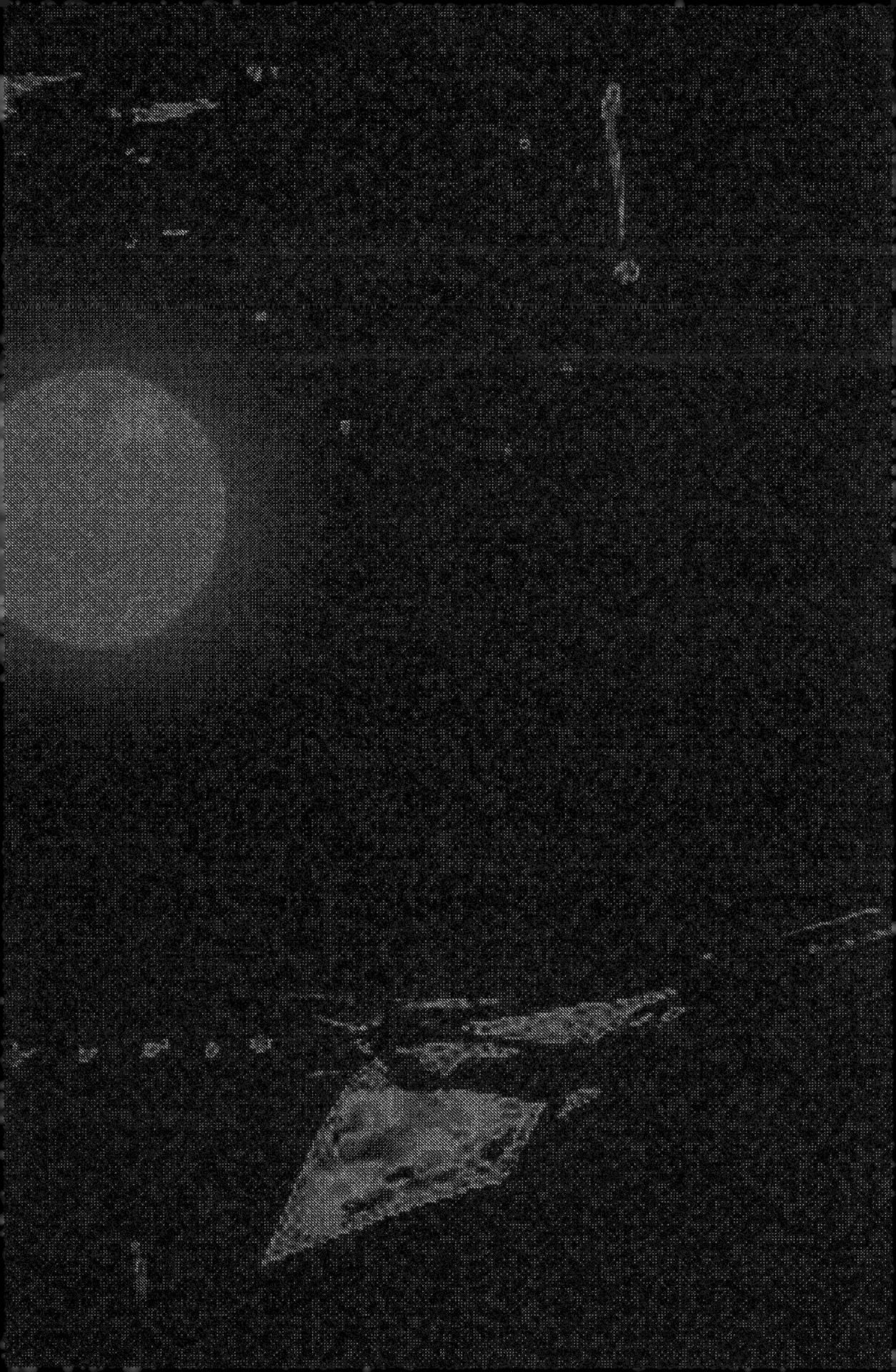

go pre

CPSIA information can be obtained
at www.ICGtesting.com
Printed in the USA
LVIC04n1315270314
379201LV00003B/3